BRITAIN IN OLD PHOTOGRAPHS

HARROW, STANMORE & PINNER

DON WALTER

SUTTON PUBLISHING LIMITED

Sutton Publishing Limited
Phoenix Mill · Thrupp · Stroud
Gloucestershire · GL5 2BU

First published 1996

Cover photographs: (front) St Ann's Road, Greenhill, *c.* 1912; (back) the High Street, Harrow on the Hill, *c.* 1900.

British Library Cataloguing in Publication Data
A catalogue record for this book is available from the British Library.

ISBN 0-7509-1075-5

Typeset in 10/12 Perpetua.
Typesetting and origination by Sutton Publishing Limited.
Printed in Great Britain by Ebenezer Baylis, Worcester

CONTENTS

St Mary's Church, Harrow on the Hill, from the lower churchyard, *c*. 1929.

INTRODUCTION

Like London itself, the present London Borough of Harrow is less a homogeneous whole than a string of former separate village communities, each with its own impressive history. Although Brockley Hill in Stanmore is widely accepted as the site of the Roman station of *Sulloniacae*, the early history of the area really begins on the heights of Harrow Hill around the time of Domesday Book, William the Conqueror's 1086 record of his conquest.

By then, the Manor of Harrow, known as Herges, had been in the keeping of the Archbishops of Canterbury for over 260 years and had a population of around 500 souls. It may even have had an early church – certainly Domesday makes mention of a priest – long before William's friend Archbishop Lanfranc founded the present St Mary's in 1087.

If the presence of a church helped to bring substance and stability to the community, it was a later foundation, Harrow School, that brought a still-enduring fame. Once again, the evidence points to an

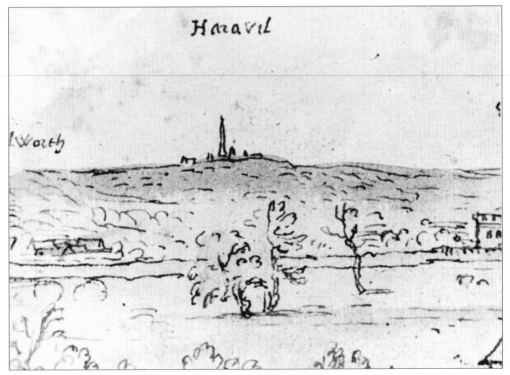

Greatly enlarged detail from the first known drawing of Harrow Hill, here called Haravil; the drawing was commissioned by Phillip II of Spain prior to his marriage to Mary Tudor in 1554.

earlier, perhaps church, school on the Hill, but the Harrow School we know today dates from the charter which yeoman farmer John Lyon of nearby Preston was granted by Queen Elizabeth I in 1571.

Lyon undoubtedly intended his foundation to be a free local grammar school; however, a loophole in the school's statutes combined with the unsuitability of its purely classical curriculum for local farmers' and tradesmens' sons, enabled it to attract more wealthy 'foreigners'. These subsequently included Lord Byron, Richard Brinsley Sheridan and no fewer than seven future prime ministers, most notably Winston Churchill. Happily, the continued presence of the School, and the existence of conservation bodies such as the Harrow Hill Trust has ensured fewer changes to the Hill townscape than to any other part of the Borough.

Pinner High Street is another interesting survival, still dominated by the Church of St John, rebuilt and reconsecrated as early as 1321. More amazingly, Pinner's High Street still plays host to an annual fair first granted by royal charter in 1336.

Whereas Pinner was once part of the manor and parish of Harrow, the no less historic district of Stanmore has maintained its own identity, at least from the time of Domesday. Originally, there were two Stanmores, Magna and Parva; just to confuse matters, Stanmore Parva was sometimes known as Whitchurch. It was within the latter's boundaries that the profligate Duke of Chandos built his even more profligate mansion, Canons, around 1713. He also rebuilt the church of St Lawrence, where he employed as organist no less a musician than 'the great Mr Handel'. Though Canons has long since disappeared, the interior of the church remains as a virtually unique example of English Baroque decoration. Greater Stanmore's church is also unusual in that the present building (consecrated 1850) was built within the grounds of the old (consecrated 1634) which still survives as a picturesque ruin.

How then did these small communities, surrounded by mile after mile of farmland, become today's busy Borough? The answer in Harrow, as elsewhere, really begins with the coming of the railroad, or to be more precise, with the choice in 1837 of rural Wealdstone as a station on the new London to Birmingham Railway. Forty-three years later, the district known as Greenhill, at the foot of Harrow Hill, also acquired a station (on the Metropolitan Line). Inevitably, this brought yet more residents into the area whose name and fame had been carried far afield by the continued growth of Harrow School throughout the nineteenth century.

The Hill thus managed to remain the focus of local business, social and administrative life until around the outbreak of the First World War. Ultimately, however, so much development in so confined an area meant that businesses and institutions were obliged to move down the Hill, to the new parish of Greenhill, if they were to have any chance of further expansion. In the meantime, Greenhill's neighbour Wealdstone, aided by its vital railway link, had attracted many important manufacturers, notably Kodak Ltd (established in Harrow in 1890), and was fast becoming an important community in its own right.

Similar expansion occurred on the other side of the Hill in ancient Roxeth, after the Roxeth Gas Works had been established in about 1855. Roxeth's growth was further accelerated by the opening in 1903 of a station on the District Line. For convenience, the station was named South Harrow and, to the dismay of older residents, this name quickly replaced the original Roxeth, certainly for the tens of thousands who flocked to all parts of Harrow during the great inter-war building boom.

But if development in Harrow tended to mark time for the next few decades, Harrow's planners and developers are certainly making up for it today; indeed, anyone currently visiting the 'town centre' area after only a fifteen or twenty year absence would find it totally and irrevocably transformed. Practical, sensible people will tell you that this transformation has brought a positive gain to the town, not least in commercial vigour and vitality. That there has also been a definable loss is equally without dispute – as the following pages reveal.

HARROW ON THE HILL

Lithograph by Nathaniel Whittock depicting the High Street, Harrow on the Hill, c. 1830. By this time, the High Street was already taking recognizable shape, dominated at its highest point by the town's oldest and most important buildings. On the left is St Mary's, the parish church consecrated in 1094, and in the centre are the original buildings of Harrow School, founded by Royal Charter in 1571.

Both friend and archbishop to William the Conqueror, Archbishop Lanfranc is commemorated in a Victorian stained glass window in the tower of St Mary's which he founded in 1087. Sadly, he died before its consecration which was performed in 1094 by his successor, Archbishop (later Saint) Anselm. A jealous Bishop of London is alleged to have jeopardized the ceremony by arranging for the theft of one of the holy vessels.

After more than 900 years only the foundations of Lanfranc's original church survive. The arch above the west door is now the oldest part of the building and reveals characteristic Norman ornamentation. The battered wooden door of somewhat later date leads into the belfry, which was at one time used to house the parish fire engine.

Engraving of the West door of St Mary's Church, 1810. The addition of the now-famous spire in about 1450 required the subsequent strengthening of the tower by vast buttresses that remain to this day. The spire was the principal glory of an ambitious rebuilding programme by the fifteenth-century rector John Byrkhede, whose lavishly detailed brass is among the church's most interesting possessions.

The rebuilding of the bell frame in 1960 provided Harrovians with a rare opportunity for a close-up view of St Mary's bells, of which the oldest dates from 1654. Their number has since been increased from eight to ten, and all bear appropriate inscriptions. One of the newer bells carries a verse written by the former Poet Laureate, John Betjeman, who knew and loved St Mary's.

John Byrkhede's Tudor rebuilding included the installation of a notably fine timber roof which has survived even the depredations of the Civil War. Its most noteworthy features are twelve figures of the apostles trampling evil (in the form of tiny stone grotesques), and a number of angels, each bearing a different medieval musical instrument.

St Mary's thirteenth-century font. Although now regarded as an irreplaceable treasure, the Purbeck Marble font, made in about 1200, was thrown into the streets early in the nineteenth century to make way for what a contemporary report called 'a marble wash-hand basin-looking-thing'. The original was happily preserved in an adjoining garden and was finally restored after many years of local agitation.

The Revd John Cunningham, *c.* 1859. Between 1774 and 1897 St Mary's had only three vicars, of whom the longest serving (1811–1861) was the Revd John Cunningham, photographed here towards the end of his long life. Cunningham knew – and sometimes clashed with – all the important Harrow figures of his time, including the families of Lord Byron and Anthony Trollope.

John Lyon Memorial, St Mary's. The church and Harrow School have long enjoyed far more than a geographical closeness and in 1812 Vicar Cunningham welcomed as a gift from the School this memorial to its founder, John Lyon. Modelled by the noted sculptor John Flaxman, its figures, symbolizing the master–pupil relationship, are said to represent the head master with the three sons of Old Harrovian Spencer Perceval, the Prime Minister assassinated in office earlier that year.

This romanticized Victorian illustration shows the view from St Mary's Terrace towards Windsor. The presence of a schoolboy is undoubtedly inspired by the fact that Lord Byron, as a schoolboy at Harrow, used to lie and scribble on the so-called Peachey Stone, which he described as his 'favourite spot'. At the end of the last century, this stone had to be protected against souvenir-hunters by a heavy metal cage, which is still in place today.

Byron's love for Harrow was such that, when his five-year-old daughter Allegra died in Italy, he asked for her to be buried and a memorial to be erected at St Mary's. Because the child was illegitimate, Vicar Cunningham allowed only a private ceremony and refused to permit a memorial to be built, and poor Allegra was virtually forgotten for 178 years until 1980 when the Byron Society placed this small marker by the south door.

When Vicar Cunningham died in 1861, the parish erected this beautiful lychgate in his memory. Contemporary opinion, however, was divided, one correspondent to the *Harrow Gazette* even urging 'some of the boys' to get out one night and pull it down. But by the end of the century, it was much in demand as a background for family photographs.

A Vicarage to St Mary's was endowed on its present site during the Primacy of Edmund Rich (1234–40), although the precise date is not known. The present Vicarage, however, is largely Victorian and, as the picture shows, extends to within a few yards of Harrow School's oldest building, the aptly called Old Schools (right).

Old Schools from an illustration of 1795. St Mary's spire overlooks the playground – or, as it is known at Harrow, the Bill Yard – of Old Schools. The very first Harrow School building, Old Schools was completed in 1615. Although ample evidence points to the existence of an earlier, probably church, school on roughly the same site, today's Harrow School springs directly from the 1571 Royal Charter obtained by John Lyon.

Old Schools and Church Hill, *c.* 1830. This charming lithograph by Harrow School drawing-master Thomas Wood shows Old Schools with the new wing that was added in 1820. Architect Charles Cockerell so cleverly matched the two wings that today they appear to be of the same age. In the 1830s, a public house called the Crown and Anchor adjoined the School gates, with Dame Armstrong's House immediately opposite.

Church Hill, early 1900s. By this time, Dame Armstrong's House (right), which was used as a School boarding house, had acquired a dense covering of ivy. The building was finally demolished after the First World War to make way for the School's handsome War Memorial buildings, designed by Sir Hubert Baker, architect of the Bank of England.

The Bill Yard, c. 1912. Cockerell's twin wings, each with its own impressive oriel window, can be clearly seen in this picture showing the roll-call ceremony known as Bill. The second School Chapel (right) towers above Dame Armstrong's House. Out of sight on the left is the so-called Milling Ground, a grassed area where scores could be settled in bare-knuckled fist fights.

The view down Church Hill to the Head Master's House, *c.* 1880. Then, as now, the building known as the Head Master's House stood at the foot of Church Hill. The present building was built in the early 1840s to designs by the celebrated Decimus Burton (designer of the Palm House at Kew Gardens), following a massive fire that destroyed its predecessor and threatened the entire village. In more recent times, the head master has chosen to make his residence in a separate private house called Peel House after Old Harrovian Sir Robert Peel.

Old Schools and the adjoining Crown and Anchor public house seen from the gardens of the Vaughan Library, which was designed in 1863 by the noted Victorian architect George Gilbert Scott. The library was named after Charles Vaughan, whose fifteen years as head master saw a spectacular growth in the School's size and reputation.

Shaftesbury plaque, Church Hill. For the past hundred years, a plaque on the wall by Old Schools has commemorated not only the great Victorian philanthropist, Lord Shaftesbury, but also the event that allegedly changed his life. It was here that, as a schoolboy, he witnessed a funeral so impoverished that he decided to devote his life to the relief of the poor and needy.

The first Harrow School Chapel, *c.* 1839. As Harrow School grew, its numbers put such pressure on the seating accommodation at St Mary's that in 1839 the School built a small chapel to designs by Charles Cockerell. However, the formidable Vicar Cunningham claimed that this was contrary to the wishes of the School's founder and for decades the boys were obliged to alternate their attendance between church and chapel.

The second School Chapel, photographed before 1920. When the School outgrew its first chapel, George Gilbert Scott was commissioned to create this building which, with many additions, is still in use today. The busy and successful Scott was considered a particularly suitable choice for in the previous decade he had completely restored St Mary's.

Outside Speech Room, schoolboys and guests await the arrival of the Prince and Princess of Wales (later King Edward VII and Queen Alexandra) on Speech Day, 1894. Speech Room, the School's principal place of assembly, was built to magnificent if rather idiosyncratic designs by William Burges between 1874 and 1877. It is said that the entire School Building Committee resigned when Burges unveiled his plans.

Church Hill, *c*. 1926. The School War Memorial building, honouring the 649 Old Harrovians who died in the First World War, stands in the centre. On the left is one of the many parades of shops which once made Harrow Hill the principal shopping centre of the district. The shops were later pulled down, allowing a better view of both Old Schools and Druries, a handsome boarding house which had been virtually hidden since its erection in 1864.

Some four years after ascending the throne, King Edward VII and his Queen returned to Harrow in 1905. Crowds lined an elaborately decorated High Street to watch the procession. The King's carriage has just passed the Hill's first bank, the London and Home Counties, which, together with its successors, remained at the same High Street premises until 1995.

Harrow fire station, c. 1880. In 1880 the Hill acquired its first purpose-built fire station at the junction of High Street and the very steep Byron Hill Road. Since the pump was horse-drawn, this site was also conveniently close to the stables of the King's Head Hotel (right), which was paid by the fire brigade to have horses ready at a moment's notice.

Harrow fire brigade, *c*. 1883. The volunteer fire brigade are shown here with members of the Harrow
Local Board in the gardens of the Harrow School boarding house, The Park. The little boy on the far left is
the 'caller', whose job it was to knock up those firemen who were unlikely to have heard the fire alarm.
The Hill's fire station remained in active service until 1963, a fact now commemorated by a plaque on the
premises, currently occupied by an estate agent.

Although instantly recognizable today, this view of the High Street was in fact taken in about 1875 when, as the mid-road pile of horse-manure indicates, the very limited traffic was exclusively horse-drawn. A further clue to the picture's date lies in the just-visible canopy sheltering the town well at the top of West Street, which remained in operation until 1879.

Drinking fountain, High Street, c. 1980. Today, the site of the old town well is marked by a (disused) drinking fountain which was presented to the town by T.C. Hudson, a local businessman. It was erected in 1880, a year after the well had been finally sealed. During the nineteenth century there was another well in use at the top of Grove Hill.

High Street, *c.* 1900. In Victorian and Edwardian days, Harrow Hill was the principal shopping centre of the area with shops lining the High Street. The 1850 *Handbook For Visitors*, which conveniently, if snobbishly, identified residents as either 'gentry' or 'traders', was able to list no fewer than a hundred names in the latter category.

The King's Head Hotel, *c.* 1960. Conveniently located at the very heart of Harrow Hill, with a pleasant green by its front door, the King's Head Hotel has served the community for several centuries although there is no recorded evidence to support the date of 1535 that for many years was painted on its façade. Sadly, the hotel lost its licence in recent times and is currently used as a social services hostel.

The Grove, c. 1986. Now one of Harrow School's eleven principal boarding houses, The Grove was once the home of the Barons Northwick, Lords of the Manor of Harrow. In 1781 an earlier house on the site was leased by the playwright Richard Brinsley Sheridan, who had formed a strong attachment to Harrow during his years there as a schoolboy. Only the demands of his joint theatrical and political career ultimately obliged him to move from Harrow to Mayfair.

The Park, from a nineteenth-century drawing. With its graceful architectural proportions, magnificent views and gardens designed by Capability Brown, The Park in London Road ranks as one of the Hill's grandest houses. Once the private residence of the 2nd Baron Northwick, the house has been in Harrow School's hands since the 1830s and is now a major boarding house. Maud Montgomery, the mother of Lord Montgomery, was brought up at The Park, where her father was house-master, at the end of the nineteenth century.

Flames and smoke burst from the windows of West Acre, the Harrow School boarding house in London Road, during the fire of 4 April 1908 which ultimately gutted the building. Good fortune ensured that its boarders were attending Speech Room at the time. Good management enabled its rebuilding, to virtually the same design, within a matter of months.

A peaceful London Road, photographed from outside West Acre in about 1930. The family on the right are passing a stable-like structure which is said to have housed auxiliary horses for the use of the horse-drawn fire brigade early in the twentieth century.

Manor Lodge, London Road, *c.* 1950. Until its demolition in the 1950s, Manor Lodge was undoubtedly the most ornate house in London Road. Designed by the gifted Edwin Prior, whose reputation extended far beyond his native Harrow, it was for many years the home of Dr H. Crichton Miller, the pioneer psychologist and founder of the Tavistock Clinic.

Woodbridge's and the Poor House, West Street, *c.* 1890. The staff of Woodbridge's, plumbers and builders, line up outside the West Street premises. Harry Woodbridge himself is said to have tended Winston Churchill's burns when, as a schoolboy, the latter used a home-made bomb to clear a well in the grounds of nearby Roxeth House (*see* page 116). The building on the right was once Harrow's Poor House.

The Cricketers, West Street, *c.* 1930. Around the turn of the century – and beyond – the Hill could lay claim to almost as many drinking places as shops; The Cricketers was one of nine licensed premises and four off-licences within a quarter-mile radius. Its name was inspired by its proximity to the School's cricket fields. The property is now a private house.

Crampton's Refreshment Rooms, West Street, *c.* 1914. Crampton's was typical of the small shops that once packed the Hill end of West Street. Kelly's Trade Directory for 1915–16 lists as its neighbours George Fletcher, cycle-maker, and Rabjohn, straw hat maker, the latter being an especially prosperous business in a town whose school population was – and still is – required to wear straw boaters.

The view along West Street towards the cricket fields, *c.* 1900. Part of the Hill's original nucleus of streets (the others being High Street and Crown Street), West Street still retains its Victorian look. The red-brick Mission House (right) is virtually unaltered in appearance, but is now used as a plastics factory; it also incorporates a rare medieval survival (*see* below).

The Pye House, off West Street. This little building with its half-timbered gable is all that remains of Harrow's medieval court-house. Built as a means of dispensing justice to those participating in the fairs and markets on the adjoining Church Fields, it acquired the name Pye Powder House. A corruption of the Norman-French 'pied poudre', the name was inspired by the dusty feet of those who came here seeking justice at a time when the roads were no more than cart-tracks.

The cricket fields from Lower Road, 1874. Sporting activities at Harrow School have ensured the survival of a 'girdle of green' around Harrow Hill; the Sixth Form Cricket Ground is an especially attractive example. The view of West Street's cottages and St Mary's Church looks very little different today.

This idyllic view of Yew Walk Cottages, off West Street, has been lost in recent years owing to the building of Harrow School's new Ryan Theatre and, more controversially, a small estate of modern houses. Most local residents had previously assumed that these open spaces belonged to the local authority when in fact they were actually leased from the true owners, Harrow School.

Once a problem for the mail coach, Harrow Hill's steepness proved even more disastrous for this Daimler Wagonette which broke its back wheel while negotiating the bend at the bottom of Grove Hill in 1899. The driver and one of his passengers lost their lives, earning a place in automotive history as the very first fatalities in a petrol-driven car. The car had been on a test run for the Army and Navy Stores, which were then contemplating switching their deliveries from horse-drawn wagons to motor cars. Exactly seventy years later, in 1969, Harrow's Mayor, Charles Stenhouse (below, left), unveiled a plaque commemorating the accident. Perhaps as a warning to drivers to curb their speed, the plaque was placed not at the scene of the accident but at the top of Grove Hill.

In 1921 an area at the bottom of Grove Hill was set aside for the town's war memorial, shown here at its unveiling by Lord George Hamilton, Chairman of the Governors of Harrow School who had donated the land. Earlier, in a more agricultural age, the site had been used as the town pound to which all stray animals were brought.

View towards Windsor, c. 1928. This novel composite picture of the view from Harrow Hill shows the unimpeded vista of the late 1920s, with (inset) the towering gas holders that later dominated the skyline. Happily, the latter were finally removed in 1986, making the view once again one of the finest in Middlesex.

Claimed to be beyond repair, this crumbling tower in the grounds of St Dominic's Convent School in Mount Park Road was pulled down in the mid-1960s even though experts had identified it as a genuine Armada Tower from the reign of Queen Elizabeth I. The school, now a sixth form college, has an equally interesting history, developing from a convent established in 1878 by nuns of the Third Order of St Dominic who were invited to Harrow by the great Catholic churchman and Old Harrovian, Cardinal Manning.

After a somewhat controversial planning decision, the building on the left – once the convent of the Little Sisters of Mercy, on Sudbury Hill – has been replaced by a vast apartment block. The adjoining chapel, being the work of George Gilbert Scott, was spared demolition. Deconsecrated, it currently serves as a sports and recreation centre.

Harrow Cottage Hospital, Roxeth Hill, 1906. Seen during its construction in 1906, Harrow's first purpose-built hospital was the work of the much-admired local architect Arnold Mitchell, who also built Hampstead's University College Schools and London's Mayfair Hotel. His hospital, most recently used for the care of the elderly sick, is threatened with closure since most of its functions are now filled by Northwick Park Hospital in Watford Road, built in 1970 (*see* page 55).

Situated at the end of a long private road that shares its name, Julian Hill was built by Thomas Trollope, father of the famous literary family, on land he had leased from Lord Northwick in 1819. Later, a decline in the family's fortunes forced the young Anthony Trollope to move to a tumbledown farmhouse in Harrow Weald, about which he wrote bitterly in his autobiography. Julian Hill still remains a private residence.

Station Road, Harrow, *c.* 1920. The transformation of the lowland rural hamlet of Greenhill into today's Central Harrow was greatly accelerated in about 1899 when Peterborough Road, the main road leading off Harrow Hill, was linked to the former Greenhill Lane. Rechristened Station Road, the latter quickly filled with villas (shown here), with shops on the opposite side.

Station Road, *c.* 1950. Photographed around thirty years after the picture reproduced above, the junction of Station Road with Kenton Road is still relatively quiet in comparison with today. The open space on the corner has been preserved, to some extent, by its use as a nursery and garden centre. At the junction, Station Road becomes Peterborough Road, named after a Harrow School head master who, on leaving the School, was appointed Dean of Peterborough.

CENTRAL HARROW

Central Harrow, as it is known today, sprang from the small hamlet (later parish) of Greenhill. Its growth was hastened by the opening in 1880 of a station on the Metropolitan Railway, seen here from the air in about 1923. Originally called Harrow station, its name was subsequently — and somewhat inaccurately — changed to Harrow on the Hill, the name it bears to this day.

College Road, 1908. A steam train puffs its way towards Pinner in this winter's day photograph of College Road, which had its own entrance to Harrow Metropolitan station. The other, busier, entrance was in Lowlands Road which gave direct access to Harrow Hill, then the centre of local life.

In the 1920s College Road was still largely residential. A large sign between the houses (right) pointed the way to what was then known in full as the Metropolitan and Grand Central Railway station. Although College Road was ultimately to have a college (Heathfield School) of its own, the original name is believed to have been bestowed as a gesture of courtesy towards the famous 'college' on the Hill.

Station Road, *c.* 1912. A second giant station sign stood at the Hill end of Station Road which, in the years immediately prior to the First World War, was already becoming one of the district's premier shopping streets. The half-timbered property in the centre of the picture is still in use as a shop.

Station Approach, Harrow. Brentnall & Cleland, coal merchants, were among those occupying small but well patronized lock-up shops on the immediate approach to Harrow 'Met' station. Others included T.D. & A.R. Pearsey, estate agents, and early branches of Finlays, the tobacconists, and W.H. Smith's.

College Road post office, before 1963. The post office was one of the first public services to move from what the *Harrow Gazette* called 'the scholastic heights' down the Hill to Greenhill where, in 1914, these handsome premises in College Road were opened. A new and much larger post office was built on the same site in the 1960s.

College Road, *c.* 1950. College Road maintained its pleasant market town atmosphere for several decades until the building boom of the 1970s. Today, both the church tower (right) and the ornate portico of the bank (centre) have long since vanished.

College Road Baptist Church, 1978. This roof-top view shows the original Baptist Church, which opened in 1908, with, beyond, some of the buildings belonging to the 1963 post office. In 1982 the church was demolished and then rebuilt as part of an ambitious multi-purpose development.

Station Approach, c. 1979. Although these particular lock-up shops vanished in the 1980s with the building of a large bus terminal, other shops were built into the new enclosed station forecourt. The low brick building visible in the gap between the station entrance and the shops is substantially the same electricity sub-station that can be seen in the 1920s aerial view (see page 35).

Shops in Station Road near the junction with St Ann's Road, *c.* 1895. Shortly after this photograph was taken, the private houses on the right also acquired shop-fronts. Early traders included Lidstones, a butcher's with its own slaughter-house nearby, and the confectionery business of J. Wright Cooper; this later expanded to include the Gayton Rooms, which for decades was the town's most popular venue for wedding receptions, meetings and masonic functions.

Station Road, *c.* 1920. By the outbreak of the First World War, the local traders had been joined by many of the big chain retailers including Boots and Sainsbury's. There was also a luxury cinema, the Coliseum (right), later transformed into a theatre staging opera and ballet as well as West End tours and an annual pantomime.

Station Road junction with Lyon Road, *c.* 1920. The graceful architecture of the Coliseum, with its two distinctive minarets, dominates this aerial view. Lyon Road, running behind the theatre, was then lined with substantial villas, which have long since been replaced by impersonal office blocks.

The junction of Lyon Road and Gayton Road, before 1914. The Gayton Hall Restaurant and Bars occupy this site today. Currently, on the opposite side of the road is the Gayton Road public library, whose decorations include vast murals based on photographs taken in the early 1960s. Even a quick glance at the latter reveals the extent to which the town has changed during the last thirty-five years.

Harrow Technical College, Station Road, *c.* 1925. The large red-brick building behind the trees on the left is Harrow Technical College and School of Art. Built in 1901, it was demolished in the 1970s when the College moved to new and grander premises in the Watford Road. The College has since been absorbed into the new University of Westminster.

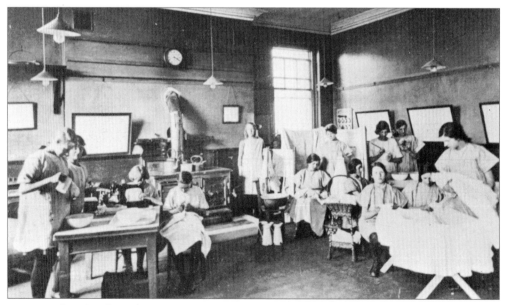

Harrow Technical College class, 1923. When the author first showed this picture, uncaptioned, in a local exhibition, it was promptly identifed by Pinner resident Ivy Field as a mothercare class 'at Harrow Tech' in 1923. Mrs Field's knowledge sprang from personal experience – she is the fair-haired girl filling a bottle on the extreme left.

Harrow Observer Printing Works, Station Road, *c.* 1930. For much of the twentieth century, the still flourishing local paper, the *Harrow Observer*, had a large printing works in Station Road, adjoining, to its reporters' great satisfaction, the Havelock Arms public house. In 1921 the paper had merged with an even older rival, the *Harrow Gazette*, which began publication on Harrow Hill in 1855.

Station Road junction with High Mead, *c.* 1960. Much has changed since this aerial view of Station Road was taken. Wealdstone Football Club's ground (centre) now houses a gigantic Tesco supermarket. The cinema in the right foreground, the 2,500-seater Dominion, was subsequently split into two small cinemas and a bingo hall. Now rechristened the Safari, it shows only Asian films.

College Road junction with Station Road, 1937. This picture reveals a Harrow that many people still recall with affection. In addition to the Harrow Coliseum (centre foreground), it shows a number of popular but long-vanished shops including the Home and Colonial, Boots (complete with lending library), a Lyons tea shop and an old-fashioned Sainsbury's grocers shop. At the top of the picture are all the many buildings, including Greenhill School, that were demolished to make way for the vast St Ann's Centre and the largely rebuilt St Ann's Road.

Manor Parade, Station Road, 1937. The 1937 aerial survey recorded the stretch of Station Road between Bonnersfield Lane and Elmgrove Road at a time when finishing touches were being put to the present Manor Parade of shops, named after the old Manor House that stood on what became the Granada Cinema site. The house behind the Parade is The Firs, where the still surviving girls' school, St Margaret's, was founded.

Bonnersfield Lane was the scene of a burst water main which provided harmless entertainment for a sizable group of spectators in August 1906. This same site became a true entertainment centre thirty years later when movie star Jessie Matthews opened the Granada (now the ABC) Cinema. With over 2,200 seats, the Granada originally boasted more seating than Harrow's new nine-screen multiplex.

The first St John's Church, Greenhill, *c.* 1866. Although Greenhill did not become a parish in its own right until 1896, it gained its first Anglican Church as early as 1866. Designed by Bassett Keeling, its somewhat Italianate styling included a separate bell-tower whose curious conical-shaped roof earned it the nickname 'the candle snuffer'. For some thirty years, St John's was administered from St Mary's, Harrow on the Hill.

St John's first vicar, the Revd Tommy Smith, made it his life's work to build a new and finer church and in 1904 this handsome building arose on the same impressive corner site. This picture, taken in about 1908, shortly after its opening, shows the west end of the building, now obscured by shops, as well as the original Victoria Hall, used for all kinds of local meetings and entertainments.

Variously known as Kenmare or The White House, this substantial property in Station Road made way in 1914 for Harrow's first department store, named after its founder, W.J. Soper. Although the latter died in the 1917 influenza epidemic, the store prospered throughout the twenties and thirties and, greatly enlarged, is today's Debenhams.

Soper's department store dominates the middle ground of this aerial view dating from about 1965. Before the end of the decade, an ambitious extension had swallowed up the adjacent property, including the Marquis of Granby public house and Cakebread and Robey, builders' merchants. The store's name was then changed to Debenhams.

Appropriately enough for a road that subsequently gave its name to Harrow's first undercover shopping centre, St Ann's Road has been primarily a shopping street for most of this century. Even during the first decade, many of its original houses were already being used for commercial purposes by companies such as the brewers, Watney Combe Reid.

Many major retailers were well established in St Ann's Road by 1908. Some, like J. Axon & Co., ironmongers, took advantage of the era's relative lack of rules by staging substantial displays of their wares outside on the pavement.

The Picturedrome, Clarendon Road, *c.* 1912. In 1910 the Clarendon Road end of St Ann's Road became the site of Greenhill's first cinema, the grandly named Empire and Picturedrome. Unlike earlier cinemas in nearby Wealdstone, it was not a financial success and closed in 1913; however, the Royal Oak public house (right) is still open for business in 1996.

Adams Furniture Stores, Clarendon Road. After minor alterations to its façade, the Picturedrome became Adams Furniture Stores; its spacious interior and shop windows on three out of four sides are still fondly remembered by local shoppers. The store was ultimately demolished as part of the overall St Ann's Centre development.

The use of St Ann's Road as part of an ill-fated one-way traffic system in October 1967 merely resulted in bumper-to-bumper traffic jams. This scene contrasts strongly with today's pedestrian precinct which now leads past the St Ann's Centre to Harrow's newest acquisition, the massive St George's Centre.

Whatever its gains, the relatively recent redevelopment of Central Harrow has meant the loss of once-popular roads. Clarendon Road, now reduced to a kind of canyon between an office block and a multi-storey car park, was once a much-frequented shopping street linking Station Road and St Ann's Road. Somertons, on the extreme right, was then the town's most admired fashion shop.

Another street dramatically changed by redevelopment is Springfield Road, which has lost all the tiny shops depicted here, as well as Adams Furniture Store (*see* page 49), the rear of whose premises is visible on the far right. These changes have rendered the area virtually unrecognizable to anyone who had left Harrow some twenty years ago.

Lowlands, a Georgian villa still surviving at the heart of the present Greenhill College complex, gave its name to the adjoining Lowlands Road, pictured here before the First World War. The curious building on the left was a lodge to the Lowlands Estate. It was occasionally used as a court-house when Lowlands was occupied by barrister and magistrate, Benjamin Rotch.

A reminder of Greenhill's agricultural past, Honeyburn Farm was one of a number of working farms in the immediate area. Situated off Bessborough Road, it survived until the 1920s, when its fields formed the basis of the Charles Crescent council estate. Happily, nearby Roxeth Farm has been preserved through conversion into a pair of handsome private houses.

Though in appearance the Kingsfield Arms public house in Bessborough Road remains virtually unchanged, most of the other buildings in this tranquil turn-of-the-century scene have long since vanished and the road is now one of the busiest in the Borough. It is named after the 6th Earl of Bessborough, a notable figure in the history of Harrow School cricket.

Harrow Swimming Baths, Charles Crescent, *c.* 1930. Opened in 1923, the former public swimming pool in Charles Crescent off Bessborough Road proved to be the most popular pool for miles around due to its pleasantly landscaped lawns and its delightful view of St Mary's. Previously, Harrow's townsfolk had been allowed to swim at Harrow School's outdoor pool, Ducker, during school vacations.

Having remained virtually unchanged throughout the 1940s and 1950s, Greenhill really began its transformation into today's Central Harrow in the following decade. Here, in 1963, the camera records a key moment of change as the handsome old villas of St John's Road give way to the first of the present towering office blocks.

Northwick Park golf course, 1966. Until the 1960s much of the old Northwick Park Estate, named after the Barons Northwick, sometime Lords of the Manor of Harrow, remained either as open space or as the Northwick Park golf club. But in 1966 the ground began to be cleared for the building of the town's new hospital, inevitably called Northwick Park.

Northwick Park Hospital, October 1970. Though its immediate surroundings still resembled a building site, enough of Northwick Park Hospital had been completed by the autumn of 1970 for the Queen to perform the official opening ceremony. The event attracted a large turn-out of women and children in their Sunday best; they also saw the comparatively unknown Margaret Thatcher, who attended in her capacity as Secretary of State for Education and Science.

St Ann's Centre under construction, October 1979. This building has probably done the most to change the face of Central Harrow. The photograph seems to have been taken from Havelock Place looking across to the present Marks & Spencers in St Ann's Road.

Borough Charter ceremony, Kodak Hall, 1954. A proud moment in Harrow history: the late Duke of Gloucester (centre), uncle of the Queen, presents a Charter elevating the former Urban District of Harrow to the status of a Borough. Behind the Duke is Clement Attlee, post-war Labour Prime Minister and one-time Stanmore resident.

One of the first, and most pleasant, functions of the new Borough of Harrow was to elect its first Freeman. The choice, not surprisingly, fell on the great wartime leader and Old Harrovian, Sir Winston Churchill, seen here arriving at the Kodak Hall with Lady Churchill in 1955. He received a commemorative scroll and a crystal casket made by the Wealdstone-based Whitefriars Glass company.

WEALDSTONE & HARROW WEALD

Wealdstone, sometimes described as Harrow's Victorian neighbour, largely owes its development to the fact that it was chosen as the site for the first station when the London & Birmingham Railway, seen here in a contemporary illustration, pushed its way through Harrow in 1837. Note the spire of St Mary's Church on Harrow Hill (right) whose School personnel would have preferred a station on the Wembley side of London.

Harrow View, from the 1853 Headstone Estate sale catalogue. Because of the steepness of Harrow Hill, Harrow's first railway station – now known as Harrow & Wealdstone – was inevitably some distance from the Hill community. The construction of the road now called Harrow View, however, effected what the catalogue described as 'a saving of half a mile to Harrow On The Hill from the railway station'.

Wealdstone station yard, before 1912. The Marlborough Road (rear) entrance of Harrow & Wealdstone station was used as a bus terminal while the High Street side was being rebuilt between 1911 and 1912. Of the two LNWR vehicles shown, one is bound for Watford via Harrow Weald and Bushey; the other for Greenhill. These routes, the first regular motor bus services in the area, were instituted in 1908.

Wealdstone station staff, c. 1900. Despite the arrival of the Metropolitan Line with its own station in the parish of Greenhill, the original Harrow & Wealdstone station remained popular with travellers to the City. By the early 1900s this staff photograph, appropriately posed on one of the platforms, showed some two dozen men, although this number appears to have included the cabbies and omnibus drivers who served the station.

Until Wealdstone gained a police station of its own in 1909, members of the Wealdstone and Stanmore police forces had to go to Stanmore, usually on a Wednesday, to collect their pay. On one occasion, their pay parade also provided an opportunity for a suitably solemn group photograph.

Belmont Common, 1907. Despite the development that inevitably followed the coming of the railway, there remained much open countryside in and around Wealdstone until well after the First World War. In 1907, for example, Belmont Common provided ample wild flowers for Marie Gunn and her friends to gather. Marie, whose father kept the Duck in the Pond public house, later admitted to a touch of artifice in the picture's composition, recalling that the picturesque smocks and bonnets had been specially provided for them by the photographer.

According to the recollections of many residents, street entertainers were a familiar sight in late nineteenth-century Wealdstone. Some itinerant Italians even travelled with this performing bear, pictured here in Station Road in 1896. Travelling theatres, known as 'penny gaffs', were also highly popular.

Blackberry Lane, Wealdstone, c. 1900. Blackberry Lane was apparently the local nickname for what is now Church Lane, between Wealdstone and Harrow Weald. The photographer was almost certainly Hebblewhite of 136 High Street, most of whose local street scenes feature this small girl in a floppy hat, who was, in fact, his daughter.

Junction of High Street and Spencer Road, *c.* 1913. Before the First World War, Wealdstone residents had dubbed this junction 'Doctor's Corner' after the local general practitioner, Dr Butler, who had built Ravenscroft (right) as his family home. In the 1960s Ravenscroft made way for Dauphine Court which still houses a doctor's surgery.

High Street with Trinity Villas, *c.* 1906. Ravenscroft, the house shown in the top picture, would be to the left of this peaceful High Street view which shows, on the right, Trinity Villas, now largely converted into shops, and, in the middle distance, a still-surviving shopping parade built in 1896. Its first occupants included Hurfords, printers, George Wall, florist, and Hebblewhite, the photographer, who is thought to have taken this picture.

Holy Trinity Church, Headstone Drive, 1909. In 1879 leading local families, including the Blackwells of Harrow Weald, purchased this site at the junction of High Street and Headstone Drive for the erection of Wealdstone's first parish church, Holy Trinity, consecrated in June 1881. By 1909 it had a flourishing Mothers' Union whose members posed for this commemorative photo on the occasion of their annual outing. The horses and carriages had been hired from Knotts in the High Street (*see* page 64).

One of Wealdstone's first public houses, The Case is Altered (*see* page 81), in the High Street, is pictured during the early years of the twentieth century when its neighbour was Garroway's cab yard, whose vehicles included the unusual wicker chaise seen on the far right. In 1908 the cottage to the left was pulled down to make way for Wealdstone's first – and still active – police station.

The carriage-building works of J. Knott were conveniently located in Wealdstone High Street which by the first decade of the twentieth century was already becoming a popular shopping area. Before the opening of a proper fire station in Palmerston Road in 1906, the town's fire engine was lodged at Knotts, although the only indication seems to have been the words 'Fire Station' on the lamp-post outside.

Formed in 1896, the Wealdstone fire brigade is shown here some time after its move in 1908 to the custom-built fire station in Palmerston Road. The two horses, Bob and Nancy, were almost as well known locally as the firemen for, when they were not required for brigade duties, they pulled the local refuse carts. They were named after the couple who had trained them for firefighting.

Coronet Cinema, *c.* 1911. The silent cinema appears to have made its first appearance in Wealdstone when a so-called 'Penny Bioscope' opened on the corner of High Street and Graham Road. Later known as the Wealdstone Cinema, it finally became the Coronet Cinema. Among its attractions were its own electric light plant and curtained boxes at the back, much favoured by courting couples.

The Rest Hotel, Kenton, *c.* 1907. Kenton, to the east of Harrow, is almost entirely a twentieth-century creation, much of it built by the local builder T.F. Nash in the years between the world wars. One of its few older buildings is The Rest Hotel (later the Travellers' Rest), which opened in 1900. Its tea gardens were much patronized by cyclists and ramblers for whom the opening of Kenton station in 1915 paved the way for a day out in the country.

Kodak Factory, *c.* 1960. From small beginnings in 1880, when George Eastman purchased 7 acres in Wealdstone for his first British factory, Kodak Ltd grew to be the town's biggest employers. By 1960 the world-famous photographic firm had a work-force of about six thousand, a figure considerably reduced in subsequent years. Eastman's choice of Harrow was partly based on the district's good clean air which meant that the presence of dust could be kept to a minimum in sensitive production procedures.

Kodak staff, March 1907. A group of extremely well-dressed Kodak managers pose outside one of the original Wealdstone buildings which boasts a highly decorative art nouveau-style canopy. The name of the company was emblazoned all over the façade together with an early advertising slogan – 'You press the button – we do the rest'.

Kodak Factory entrance, 1920s. By this time the company was already among the first to provide canteen, sports and social facilities. Perhaps because of the clean nature of the work, a surprisingly high percentage of Kodak workers had been women, right from the earliest days; indeed, there are many accounts of women happily walking to Kodak jobs from as far afield as South Harrow.

David Allen's printing works, *c.* 1896. Kodak's hardly less distinguished neighbour around the turn of the century was the vast printing works built in 1896 by the Belfast-based David Allen & Sons. The victim of their own success, Allen's were requisitioned by the Government in 1914 to produce ration books and other urgent wartime print. The company was never returned into private hands, instead becoming His Majesty's Stationery Office. Harrow's Crown Court now occupies much of its site.

Little Laundry, *c.* 1907. A smaller but equally successful Wealdstone business was the Little Laundry established in Stuart Road in 1907 by Miss E.B. Jayne, photographed with the pony and trap in which she usually travelled to work. Seven years later, on the outbreak of war, Lloyd George, the Minister of Munitions, employed her to help recruit women to work in the wartime munitions factories. She was later awarded an OBE for her wartime efforts.

Little Laundry, *c.* 1907. Under the direction of Miss Jayne, the Little Laundry quickly outgrew its name although its advertising slogan 'Little and Good' continued to be used. Later, the company was absorbed into Advance Contract Laundries who worked primarily for the major London hotels.

Following the outbreak of the First World War, men of the Seaforth Highlanders were photographed marching through Wealdstone High Street en route for the transit camp established in Harrow Weald, where Fontwell Close stands today. After a makeshift platform was constructed beside the railway sidings in Cecil Road, the soldiers later entrained directly from Wealdstone to France – and the misery of the trenches.

Schooldays as many people remember them are evoked by this atmospheric but undated photograph of Grant Road Schools whose junior department opened as early as 1870. It was originally known as High Street Schools and for many decades its playground could be seen from the High Street, to the entertainment of passers-by. In 1912, after the *Titanic* sank, the head master chalked out the great ship's measurements on the pavements so that his pupils could appreciate the scale of the disaster.

Bridge Schools, *c.* 1902. From September 1902 children living on the far side of Wealdstone railway bridge were educated in this highly institutional-looking block inevitably called Bridge Schools. Its first pupils were largely drawn from the newly built Rosslyn Avenue, Frognal Avenue and Ferndale Terrace, as well as from the slightly older roads that made up the area known popularly as 'Poets' Corner' (*see* page 72).

After sixty-four busy years, Bridge Schools were demolished in the mid-1960s as part of the clearance programme for Harrow's new Civic Centre. In a press photograph taken on the very last day, Head Master Mr J.D. Rees waves goodbye to Edwin Holdham, one of the school's very first pupils, and Pamela Marshall, the last girl to have been admitted to the Junior School.

'Poets' Corner', 1969. Members of Harrow's Welsh community pose in national dress beside a floral clock especially created to mark the investiture of Prince Charles as Prince of Wales in July 1969. The clock was situated at 'Poets' Corner', so called because the adjacent streets – Milton Road, Shelley Road, Burns Road and Wordsworth Road – were all named after famous poets. Only Milton Road now remains, following the building of Harrow's Civic Centre.

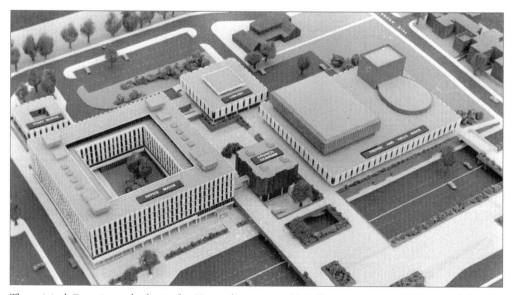

The original Georgian-style design for Harrow's post-war Civic Centre was so poorly received that the local authority agreed to hold a design competition. Of the sixty-eight final entries, this model by Eric G. Broughton was considered the best by the three very notable assessors, Sir Basil Spence, Sir Hugh Casson and Professor A. Douglas Jones. Earlier, Spence had told the local press that the winner must be a building that would give pleasure, 'not just a place in which one pays rates'.

Harrow Civic Centre shortly after its opening in 1973 and looking much as it does today. In the event, only the model's left-hand office wing and the central Council Chamber block were actually constructed, together with the library building at the rear. The town still awaits the 'theatre and halls' block. However, for the first time in Harrow's history, the Civic Centre brought together the many and varied offices that had previously been scattered throughout the Borough. For this reason alone, it was welcomed, especially as such a centre had first been discussed as long ago as 1934.

Construction of the Wealdstone underpass in June 1972 opened up this unusual view of the Civic Centre. The underpass is still in use today.

Wealdstone swimming pool, *c.* 1934. Just over a decade after the opening of Harrow's first swimming pool in Charles Crescent, Wealdstone acquired a pool of its own in Christchurch Avenue. Unlike its predecessor, it boasted night-time floodlighting and a separate paddling pool for children, yet it never quite achieved the same level of popularity.

Like most London suburbs, Wealdstone was well provided with cinemas between the world wars, with the Coronet being succeeded by the Herga, and a typical Odeon rising in Station Road. Nearby in Belmont Circle was the Plaza, later the Essoldo, seen here during its demolition in the late 1960s. The Odeon too has long since disappeared although the Herga's building has survived.

Barnard's Corner, High Street, 1958. For much of the twentieth century, W.J. Barnard's at the junction of High Street and Palmerston Road was more than a popular mens' outfitters: it was also a definite place called Barnard's Corner. Of modest size when it first opened in 1903, by 1958 Barnard's had expanded to fill the entire corner block. The site is now occupied by a fast food restaurant.

Despite some initial concern that the hill up to Harrow would prove too steep for delivery vehicles, Sainsbury's were already well established in the town before the outbreak of the First World War although their steadiest growth took place during the inter-war years. Since the company preferred a central position in the shopping parade and had created their house style as early as 1890, most branches looked exactly like this one at 483 Kingsbury Road, photographed in the mid-1930s.

Kenton Lane Farm, *c*. 1811. Though much changed from this 1811 lithograph, the principal buildings of Kenton Lane Farm still exist; indeed, the farm still operates as a milk-producing unit although the herds are maintained elsewhere. This drawing is taken from a book by the celebrated nineteenth-century horticulturist John Claudius Loudon, whose parents are buried at Pinner Church.

Kenton Lane, before the First World War. Now a busy thoroughfare connecting built-up Kenton with the hardly less developed Belmont, Kenton Lane was still very much a country lane in the first decade of this century. Much of its farmland remained in the possession of New College, Oxford, from its endowment in the early sixteenth century until the early 1930s.

The Seven Bells public house, Kenton Lane, *c.* 1912. Two Route 58 buses make a welcome stop outside the seventeenth-century public house, the Seven Bells, in Kenton Lane after their long Charing Cross to Harrow Weald run. The open-topped 'B' type vehicles were operated by London Transport's predecessor, the London General Omnibus Company.

Brazier's Dairy. The Brazier family, whose business is now based at Kenton Lane Farm, have been dairymen for nearly seventy years. Here, Mr J. Brazier lines up with members of his family and staff with their delivery floats outside the dairy premises they maintained in Kenton Park Avenue. At that time, they were able to promise 'all milk from our own cows'.

The Ballroom, Harrow Weald Park, *c*. 1945. Wealdstone's heavily wooded neighbour, Harrow Weald, remained largely undeveloped until the early nineteenth-century Enclosure Acts released considerable areas of land, promptly purchased by Londoners as 'country estates'. Among the most notable was Harrow Weald Park, at the junction of Uxbridge Road and Brookshill, whose ballroom is seen here prior to its demolition after the Second World War. Its owners included the Crockford family who operated the celebrated London gaming house of that name.

Another important house in the neighbourhood, Harrow Weald Lodge, was actually built as a public house in the early eighteenth century when it was variously called The Nag and Cold Harbour. Much altered in the last century during its conversion to a private house, it subsequently became Harrow Council offices and, at the time of writing (1996), remains in business occupation.

Grim's Dyke, *c*. 1960. Built between 1870 and 1872 by the noted architect Norman Shaw for the artist Frederick Goodall RA, Grim's Dyke achieved its greatest fame as the residence of Sir W.S. Gilbert, the librettist of Gilbert & Sullivan fame. In more recent years, it has been used as a hotel and restaurant. In 1996 there was talk of turning the estate into a Glyndebourne-style opera house with an exclusive Gilbert & Sullivan repertoire.

Grim's Dyke lake, *c*. 1911. In May 1911 Sir William Gilbert drowned in its waters: he was 74 and had apparently attempted to save a schoolgirl from drowning during a springtime bathing party.

Late nineteenth-century Harrow Weald also had its share of working farms, including Weald Farm, formerly situated at the corner of Weald Lane and High Road. At that time, High Road was home to the actor George Arliss who, following his marriage at All Saints', Harrow Weald, found success first on the London stage and later won even greater fame as Hollywood's very first Oscar-winning star.

Harrow Weald recreation ground, c. 1911. This memorial gate to the recreation ground in the High Road honours the memory of Thomas Blackwell, a famously generous member of an outstanding local family, who in 1895 gave some 15 acres to the parish for recreational use. He also rebuilt All Saints', Harrow Weald's parish church, and donated the site for St Anselm's Church, Hatch End.

The Case is Altered public house, Old Redding. In contrast to many parts of the district, Old Redding has hardly changed since this picture was taken early this century. The origin of the name remains obscure but may be linked with Thomas Redding, formerly Governor of Harrow School. The name of its public house, The Case is Altered, is equally obscure but some believe it is a corruption of the Spanish *casa alta* 'the high house' – a fitting description for a house that is, indeed, on higher ground.

'The City', Old Redding, *c*. 1930. When the local brick-making industry came into the hands of the Blackwell family early in the nineteenth century, they built a collection of cottages for their workers. The estate became known locally as 'The City' and it survived into comparatively recent times. 'The City' even had its own 'Cathedral' – the local name for The Case is Altered public house.

This peaceful street scene, perhaps taken just before the First World War, shows the junction of College Road and High Road, Harrow Weald, with an earlier Red Lion public house on the right. College Road, like other 'college' names in the vicinity, was inspired by the nearby College of St Andrew's, a short-lived venture on the part of the Old Harrovian Perpetual Curate of Harrow Weald, the Revd Edward Munro.

Although a Waitrose supermarket and a Sainsbury's Home Base DIY superstore now give a more commercial modern look to Harrow Weald High Road, the Memorial Hall and Club (right), built in 1921, still enjoys an active existence. At one time this immediate area was used as a 'dust shute' where horse-drawn carts emptied their refuse.

STANMORE

St John's Church, Stanmore. One of the oldest parts of the Borough, today's Stanmore has grown from the separate Manors of Great and Little Stanmore (also known as Whitchurch). Although each manor had its own church from medieval times, the foundation stone of the present St John's in what was formerly Stanmore Magna was laid as recently as March 1849, when the old church was declared unsafe. The ceremony was performed by Lord Aberdeen, whose son was then Rector of Great Stanmore, in the presence of the Dowager Queen Adelaide, widow of William IV. It was to prove her last public engagement from her home at Bentley Priory.

Stanmore Old Church. Although declared unsafe in the 1840s, the earlier St John's Church still survives as a picturesque ruin in the grounds of its successor. The church was consecrated in July 1632 by William Laud, Archbishop of Canterbury under Charles I. During the subsequent Civil War, Laud was charged by the Puritans that he 'outwent Papery in the consecration of chapels'; in his defence, he rightly claimed that St John's was not a private chapel but a true parish church.

St Lawrence's Church, Whitchurch. The Manor of Little Stanmore had its own church from as far back as the twelfth century but the present building largely dates from its rebuilding by the Duke of Chandos, Handel's patron, early in the eighteenth century. Though the exterior is conventional, it has a lavish baroque interior that is almost unique in Britain. During his service with the Duke, Handel not only played the church organ but also composed the famous Chandos Anthems. Whitchurch, as an alternative name for Little Stanmore, appears in various spellings from 1538 onwards.

The restoration of the interior of St Lawrence's required the church to be closed for several months in 1973 and continued throughout the decade. Here, the Mayor of Harrow and other distinguished visitors inspect the church during the course of restoration.

The so-called Lake Almshouses, which bordered the churchyard of St Lawrence's, Whitchurch, were founded in the late seventeenth century by Mary Lake, the widow of Sir Thomas Lake of Canons (*see* page 90). The almshouses were demolished in 1957 and a parish hall now stands in their place.

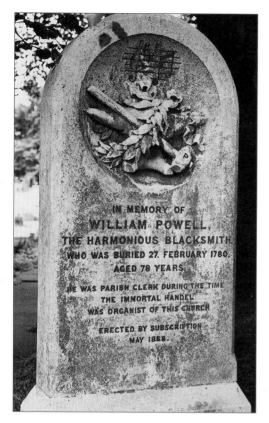

In addition to the typically Edwardian memorial to the librettist Sir William Gilbert, the churchyard of St Lawrence's, Whitchurch, houses this interesting monument put up nearly one hundred years after the death of William Powell, who had combined the roles of blacksmith and parish clerk during the years that Handel was the parish organist. It was thus assumed that he had provided the inspiration for Handel's composition, 'The Harmonious Blacksmith', overlooking the fact that this title was never used in Handel's lifetime.

London Road, Stanmore, c. 1905. Traffic in this section of London Road, now known as The Broadway, then consisted of little more than the occasional pony and trap. On the left is the old village pond and pump, and on the right the garden of a long-vanished property called The Red House.

Named after the parish church which lies at its entrance, Church Road is seen here in an undated picture, perhaps taken around the time of the First World War. Although much else has changed, the Crown Inn (left) remains in business after over 190 years.

Election day, Stanmore, 1906. The election supporters of the Hon. W. Peel pose in the cart hired to take them to the polling station. The picture was taken outside the Masons Arms on the corner of Edgware High Street and Whitchurch Lane, and the horse and dray almost certainly came from Clutterbucks, an eighteenth-century Stanmore Hill brewery which discontinued brewing some ten years later.

For centuries Stanmore Hill has been one of the principal gateways to Greater Stanmore, and has witnessed the erection of many important houses and institutions, including the Old Queen's Head where eighteenth-century Vestry meetings were frequently held. Virtually nothing, however, from this late nineteenth-century view is now recognizable.

Stanmore Hill, *c.* 1916. Though the ornate lamp and drinking fountain have disappeared, the white clapboard house (now no. 113) and the brick buildings beyond still survive on Stanmore Hill. Just visible beyond the cart on the left is the sign for the still-extant Abercorn Arms public house, where in 1814 the Prince Regent (later George IV) met with the crowned heads of France, Russia and Prussia to discuss the downfall of Napoleon.

Stanmore's postal staff pose outside the district's first purpose-built post office which had opened on Stanmore Hill in February 1893. The Postmaster was then Thomas Berwick who, like his father before him, combined his post office work with a successful grocery and wine merchants' business.

Luscombe Lodge, Stanmore Hill. Variously known as Luscombe Lodge and Robin Hill (but now more simply as 73 Stanmore Hill), this early eighteenth-century house was, around the turn of the twentieth century, the home of the naturalist Dr Edward Wilson who wrote about the birds and wildlife of The Grove and Stanmore Common. In 1912 Wilson died a hero's death with Captain Scott on the ill-fated Antarctic expedition.

Though the original mansion of the Duke of Chandos, Handel's patron, was demolished in the mid-eighteenth century, the name and fame of Canons lives on in the district known as Canons Park and in a later house, shown here in about 1930. Part of this building now belongs to the North London Collegiate School.

Once described as a Gothic masterpiece, Stanmore Hall in Wood Lane was originally a monument to the best that Victorian money could buy, including interiors designed by William Morris and tapestries by Edward Burne-Jones. In more recent times, it has been used as a nursing home and, following a serious fire, office premises. There is talk in 1996 of transforming it into luxury flats.

One of the great 'lost' houses of Stanmore, The Grove in Warren Lane achieved its peak of fame in the 1870s when it was the home of the Victorian writer and naturalist Eliza Brightwen; many of her works include illustrations of the house and its gardens. The Grove was later bought by Sir Ernest Cassell as a gift for his daughter.

During the thirty-four years that she lived at The Grove, Eliza Brightwen was able to transform its grounds into a veritable Kew Gardens, importing botanical rarities from all over the world. Following the Second World War, the estate was acquired by the General Electric Company and later housed Marconi Space & Defence Systems. The house was finally demolished in 1979.

Few houses can boast such a colourful and varied history as Bentley Priory, built during the latter part of the eighteenth century, in part to designs by the famous architect Sir John Soane. As the name suggests, the site once housed a priory of Augustinian canons. In 1936 it became the headquarters of Fighter Command, from which Air Chief Marshal Sir Hugh Dowding directed Britain's air defences during the Second World War. In 1943 he took the title of Baron Dowding of Bentley Priory.

Demolished in 1938, Stanmore Park was for some forty years during the eighteenth century the elegant home of Andrew Drummond, founder of Drummonds Bank at Charing Cross, later absorbed into the Royal Bank of Scotland. The house became a school in the twentieth century but was subsequently acquired by the Royal Air Force who permitted its demolition in 1938. The present Stanmore Park RAF Station now stands on the site.

Much changed, though happily still standing, Hill House on Stanmore Hill has been home to both the eighteenth-century scholar Samuel Parr, and the nineteenth-century retailer Charles Fortnum of Fortnum and Mason fame. Parr, who had been Sheridan's tutor while a master at Harrow School, actually opened his own school in Hill House in 1771 but the venture was short-lived.

Although it was erected in 1760, this impressive obelisk on Stanmore Common remains comparatively little known owing to encroachment by buildings of the Royal National Orthopaedic Hospital. The obelisk marks the presumed site of the battle between the Romans under Julius Caesar and the British under Cassivellaunus in 54 BC. Less than a mile away — and much better authenticated — lies the site of the Romano-British settlement of *Sulloniacae*.

Royal National Orthopaedic Hospital, *c*. 1922. Originally founded in London in 1838, the hospital that has become the Royal National Orthopaedic has been based at Stanmore since 1909. In 1922 an extension permitted the construction of these open-ended wards intended for the care of children suffering from tuberculosis.

Green Lane, Stanmore, *c*. 1910. Though it is the grand houses that inevitably take pride of place in local history books, Stanmore does not lack for attractive cottage-style buildings. This terrace, known as Clark Cottages, is situated at the top of Green Lane and, small details apart, they look very much today as they did before the First World War.

By the outbreak of the First World War, the first commercial developments (right) were beginning to transform London Road into today's shopping parades. Subsequently, Buckingham Cottage, the Georgian house in its own large grounds (left), also made way for a row of shops, appropriately called Buckingham Parade.

Bank Corner, London Road, *c.* 1980. Some sixty years later, Stanmore Broadway would be virtually unrecognizable but for the bank on the corner, now a branch of the National Westminster, although just out of the picture the old village hall, known as the Bernays Institute, still stands. In 1986 the skyline was dramatically changed by the construction of a massive office block for the Automobile Association.

Honeypot Lane, *c.* 1925. Until the late 1930s, when it began to take the shape of today's wide highway, Honeypot Lane was as rural as its somewhat curious name suggests. Several theories have been advanced about the name's origin – the most prosaic suggested that, after heavy rain, carts got stuck in the roadway, as though in honey. A more sinister opinion is that the name is a corruption of 'hangen-pytt' – in other words, the site of a gibbet.

Photographed soon after its construction in the late 1920s, Glebe Road seems to have taken its name from the former Glebe Hut or Hall in nearby Stanmore Broadway. This extension to the 1870 Bernays Institute was built after the First World War as a meeting place for working women, especially the ladies' maids employed in the great Stanmore households of that time.

Stanmore station, 1969. This photograph represents, in every sense, the end of the line for Stanmore station, opened in December 1890 and demolished just a year after this picture was taken. Never more than a branch line from Harrow, its construction was largely financed by Frederick Gordon, the entrepreneur who transformed Bentley Priory into a hotel, and hoped that improved transport would increase his hotel trade.

Belmont station during demolition, 1966. Due to the growth of housing estates in the area, an intermediate Belmont station was added to the Harrow–Stanmore line in 1932. The line was axed in 1964, and two years later, the station buildings and footbridge were demolished.

PINNER

Once part of the manor and parish of Harrow, Pinner was first mentioned in a document of 1231 and by 1336 had already been granted its now-famous annual Fair. It was traditionally held in the High Street, depicted here. This primitive drawing is of unknown provenance but is likely to be a poor copy of an 1828 sketch showing the Church of St John and the Queen's Head public house on the left.

Pinner village, *c.* 1889. A vivid impression of rural life is conveyed by this drawing of the view towards the High Street from Chapel Lane. The only truly identifiable feature is the tower of St John's Church, which was built in 1321 as a chapelry to St Mary's, Harrow on the Hill. Despite considerable local agitation, Pinner did not become a parish in its own right until 1766.

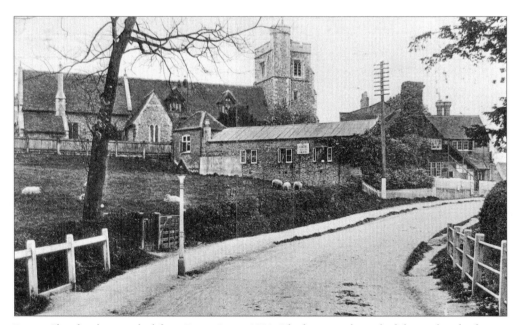

Pinner Church, photographed from Paines Lane, 1908. The house at the end of the road is the former Belle Vue which in 1878 was partially rebuilt as a Temperance tavern called The Cocoa Tree. Its adjoining fields were a favourite site for organized outings by local Sunday Schools and similar groups.

Having established themselves in Harrow by 1900, Sainsbury's, then grocers, used single-horse vans to deliver to customers in outlying districts such as Pinner. Here, in about 1925, a Sainsbury's driver pauses for a chat with a fellow vansman outside St John's Church.

Church Lane provides an attractive background for this early example of advertising which first appeared in a catalogue for Humber Tricyles. The precise date is unknown but is obviously after 1895 since the advertising copy refers to this particular machine's success in winning the 1895 One Mile Tricycle Championship, organized by the National Cyclists' Union.

Wealdstone photographer Fred Hebblewhite is known to have taken this picture of the upper High Street. The date, however, is uncertain but must be before 1898 when the gnarled town tree in front of the church finally collapsed. The two lady cyclists were probably about to enter the Queen's Head (left), then an official meeting place of the Cyclists' Touring Club.

The view down High Street, c. 1904. The fallen town tree had been replaced by a new sapling when this picture was taken from the roadway outside the sixteenth-century Church Farm whose trees can be seen on the right. The green in front of Church Farm remained private property until 1922 when it was donated to the village.

A tranquil scene in lower High Street, *c.* 1872. Two years later Eleanor Ward was knocked down and killed here by a horse that had bolted from the Queen's Head yard. Miss Ward was a descendant of Lord Nelson, being the daughter of his child by Lady Hamilton, but such was the family's seclusion in Pinner that no mention was made of the Nelson connection in the accident report.

To celebrate the Coronation in 1911 of King George V, grandfather of our present monarch, Pinner village staged a lavish carnival. Here, led by the village fire brigade, the horse-drawn procession lines up outside Gurney's, the High Street provision merchants.

Gurney's Stores, High Street. During the early years of this century, Gurney's Central Stores at 38–40 High Street was one of the district's most popular retailers, selling groceries and provisions in the main shop and wines, spirits and beers on the adjoining premises. A horse and trap, perhaps belonging to the shop's owner, wait outside.

Pinner post office staff, c. 1900. Fifteen members of staff, including a messenger boy with a bicycle, assembled for the photographer outside what was then Pinner post office at the bottom of the High Street. Over the years, the Pinner post office was run from three different High Street addresses before a custom-built brick sub-office was opened at the top of Bridge Street in 1931.

High Street, 1908. The Bazaar, a shop specializing in photographic materials, takes pride of place in this High Street picture, probably because the photograph was almost certainly taken by the shop's proprietor, Mrs Mary Emery. According to local advertisements, Mrs Emery had 'many years' West End experience as an artist and miniature painter' before opening her Pinner premises in 1908, offering an early printing service for 'amateur photographers'.

Old Parish Hall, *c*. 1960. A Pinner landmark for several decades, this attractive red-brick building at the entrance to Bridge Street served as the first National School from 1841 to 1868. After some years as a parish hall, it then became the local library. In the last few years before its demolition in 1960 it housed a number of small local businesses.

Pinner fire station and Red Lion, before 1919. The LNWR horse omnibus that ran between Pinner (Hatch End) station and Pinner village between 1885 and 1914 is seen outside two of the village's more important buildings. On the left is the old fire station at the corner of Love Lane and, on the right, the Red Lion public house which was later replaced by the present Red Lion Parade.

Junction of Chapel Lane and Bridge Street, *c.* 1900. At this time Chapel Lane still had its small narrow railway bridge, later rebuilt and widened. The row of shops on the right, including C. Jaques, stationer, newsagent and tobacconist, was the first to be built in Bridge Street. Tradesmen also occupied the wooden cottages on the left.

Another glimpse of Pinner's rural past is provided by this early twentieth-century view of the wooden signpost at the junction of Marsh Road and Eastcote Road. In more recent times, this area was known as Vagabonds' Corner after the popular meeting hall of that name. Marsh Road probably owes its name to the fact that, even in recent times, the nearby River Pinn has not infrequently overflowed its banks.

Arthur William Tooke, the son of a wealthy solicitor and Member of Parliament, had both a taste for towers and the money to indulge it. At Pinner Park Farm, which his father had purchased for him, he built three ornamental towers; the only surviving tower is seen here in an Edwardian photograph.

A substantial tower also featured in the design for Arthur William Tooke's private residence. He called it Woodhall Towers but the locals quickly dubbed it Tooke's Folly. It stood until 1965 just north of the Uxbridge Road in Hatch End and is recalled today by the name Tooke's Close, off Woodhall Drive.

Marsh Road, *c.* 1912. Pinner Baptist Chapel (right) was built on the corner of Marsh Road and Cecil Park as early as 1885 and was joined some years later by a row of houses known as Stanley Villas (later converted into shops). The chapel subsequently became Pinner's first synagogue. The first Cecil Park houses were erected by the Metropolitan Railway Surplus Land Company and had their own entrance to Pinner station.

Bridge Street, 1937. By the year of George VI's Coronation, Bridge Street, once the tranquil setting of Howard Place and Dear's Farm, had become one of Pinner's two main shopping streets. Major retailers such as Sainsbury's and Boots were among those whose businesses lined both sides of the road, seen here bedecked with Coronation decorations.

In this later view, looking down Bridge Street from Elm Park Road, the pedestrian on the left has just passed the 1899 police station (with timbered gable) and is approaching the First Church of Christ Scientist, erected in 1937. The town's only cinema, the Langham, has disappeared although the inevitable replacement supermarket has yet to arise, thus the date must be about 1981.

Waxwell Lane, named after a medieval well in the vicinity, is one of the Pinner streets which have managed to retain some of their more picturesque properties. This, for example, is the early sixteenth-century Laurel House, later rechristened Bee Cottage after the bees' nest once found in the chimney void.

Moss Lane still happily reminds us of Pinner's more leisurely past through such evocative properties as the fifteenth-century East End Farm Cottage. The lane also boasts the Five Courts, once owned by Ambrose Heal of the famous Tottenham Court Road furniture store.

Royal Commercial Travellers' School, 1947. Setting an example which other companies such as Kodak were to follow, the Royal Commercial Travellers' School was originally drawn to Harrow because of its clean, countrified air. The School, which developed into the vast complex seen here, was opened in 1855, somewhat behind schedule, by the Prince Consort who had travelled to Hatch End on the recently opened railway line. The *Harrow Gazette* unforgivingly remarked, 'From mis-management on the part of the Railway Company, some 20 minutes was lost'.

Demolition of the Royal Commercial Travellers' School, 1967. The School 'for poor and necessitous children' survived until the mid-1960s when its demolition paved the way for a vast Safeways supermarket. One of the School's principal buildings, the Elliott Hall, which dates from 1904, was saved and transformed into the Harrow Arts Centre. Its central assembly space is now successfully used as a concert hall.

Pinner & Hatch End station, c. 1897. The development of Hatch End, a northern extension of Pinner, followed the establishment of a railway station on the London–Birmingham line as early as 1842. Originally called Pinner (although that village was some mile and a half away), the station became Pinner & Hatch End in 1897. By then, the opening of both the Royal Commercial Travellers' School and the Woodridings Estate, home of cookery expert Mrs Beeton, had brought further growth to the area.

Pinner Fair, *c.* 1930. Since 1336 Pinner's street fair has taken place every year, even during wartime. Only the date has changed. Originally held on St John's Day (24 June), it has now been brought forward to the Wednesday after the Spring Bank Holiday. It is not just the crowds who return year after year; many of the showmen also have regular patches. The Pettigrew family, for example, ran the large carousel at the top of the High Street for over a century.

SOUTH HARROW

South Harrow, c. 1922. This southerly part of the Borough had been known for centuries as Roxeth. Then, in 1903, the District Railway opened a station here which they called South Harrow and, to the annoyance of older residents, the name stuck. When this aerial view was taken, the only development of any substance surrounded the Roxeth Gas Works in Northolt Road. The lane to the left is Eastcote Lane, then a quiet country lane.

Winston Churchill at Roxeth House, *c.* 1888. In one of the relatively few surviving records of Winston Churchill's years as a pupil at Harrow School (1888–92), the future Prime Minister and war leader is seen sitting on the gatepost of Roxeth House, a derelict and reputedly haunted mansion opposite Roxeth Farm in Bessborough Road. Roxeth House was demolished in 1892 and the grounds acquired for School cricket.

Northolt Road, *c.* 1905. Dressed in their Sunday best, Roxeth residents pour from the Baptist Mission Tent which was set up in 1905 in a field at Grange Farm, off Northolt Road. The intention was to develop a new Roxeth congregation to enable the existing Baptist Chapel on Roxeth Hill to move to new and larger premises in the centre of Harrow.

The Great Barn of Roxeth, *c.* 1947. One of the most imposing features of Grange Farm at Roxeth Corner was the so-called Great Barn of Roxeth. Its dimensions (100 ft long, 60 ft wide and 65 ft tall) made it among the finest in the county but did not prevent its demolition, allegedly due to bomb damage, in the late 1940s.

Nobes' Forge, Roxeth Corner, *c.* 1900. When Roxeth was still primarily an agricultural community, George Nobes (right, in bowler hat) ran a successful forge and wheelwrights business at Roxeth Corner adjacent to the Timber Cart public house. After rebuilding, the latter was given its present and rather more grandiose name, the Timber Carriage.

The Half Moon public house, Roxeth Corner, before 1893. There is still a Half Moon public house on the site today but this is its predecessor, a conversion from two cottages at the foot of Roxeth Hill. In 1862 it was licensed to Abraham Farmborough, whose family also owned the recently demolished Roxborough Tavern in Harrow.

Roxeth Corner, c. 1908. The rebuilt Half Moon public house dominates this picture of Roxeth Corner which, during the early years of the twentieth century, was regarded as the village centre of Roxeth. Its well-patronized shops included Wingroves, butchers, and Sladdens, occupying two adjacent properties, a drapers shop that can lay some claim to being Harrow's first department store.

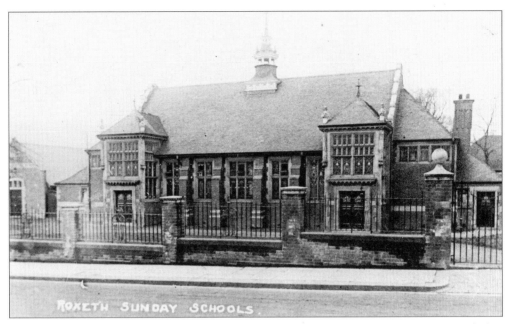

Roxeth's Christ Church had been built more than half way up the very steep Roxeth Hill, and therefore there was a need for a parish building nearer the village centre. This was first met in 1881 by a small Mission Hall in Northolt Road. This was followed seventeen years later by a much grander parish hall on the opposite side of the road. This parish hall remained until 1978 when it made way for an office block.

By the end of the Second World War, Roxeth Corner was already undergoing a transformation. Within a few more years, the remaining farmland and farm buildings, including the Great Barn of Roxeth, would all vanish beneath the creation of the Grange Farm Estate.

South Harrow station, before 1935. The original South Harrow station, whose opening in 1903 did so much to transform the area, still stands today in South Hill Avenue. District Line carriages operated here until 1933 when they were replaced by Piccadilly Line tube trains. Two years later, a new station was built a few hundred yards away in Northolt Road.

A likely contender for the title of Harrow's most changed road, Northolt Road is seen here some time after the railway station and adjoining bridge were opened in 1903. The street was then lined with small cottages and shops, of which only a couple near the station have survived. In mid-1996 the road was further altered to accommodate a Waitrose superstore.

The opening of the well-staffed Harrow School Laundry in Alma Road encouraged the building of many small shops at the Roxeth Corner end of Northolt Road, many of which survived until the 1950s. Of the buildings shown here in about 1950, only the British Legion Club (with clock) still stands.

The Three Horseshoes, Roxeth's oldest public house, first licensed in 1730, stood next to the Roxeth Gas Works in Northolt Road. Although the latter's workers were forbidden to enter its doors during working hours, many were known to slip over the adjoining wall for 'a quick one'. The pub was demolished in 1961.

With the consecration of Christ Church, Roxeth Hill, in July 1862, Harrow added to its legacy of buildings by George Gilbert Scott. This noted Victorian architect had already worked on the restoration of St Mary's Church, Harrow on the Hill, and designed both the Chapel and the Vaughan Library for Harrow School. In a bold but successful contemporary design Christ Church has recently integrated the church with a suite of parish meeting rooms.

Roxeth Hill School, from an engraving of *c.* 1851. Opened in 1812 as the first real local alternative to Harrow School, the subsequent progress of Roxeth Hill School was greatly helped by the generosity of the great Victorian philanthropist Lord Shaftesbury. In 1851 he gave this building to the School in memory of his son Ashley, who had died while a pupil at Harrow School. Surrounded by more modern buildings, the 1851 block is still in use.

Welldon Park School, *c.* 1912. Twenty-six small children were persuaded to sit still with their hands behind their backs for this Class Two photograph taken shortly after the opening of the School in 1912. This was the first school to serve the rapidly developing streets around the new South Harrow station.

The Paddocks pleasure grounds, Northolt Road, *c.* 1912. In the first decades of the twentieth century, a summertime treat for children and grown-ups alike was a trip to The Paddocks pleasure ground, complete with miniature railway, that had been created from the former Grove Dairy Farm in Northolt Road. Much of The Paddocks is still open space for in the 1930s many of its 30 acres formed the basis of the local authority's Alexandra Park.

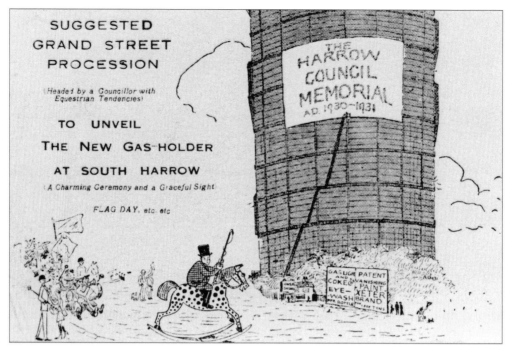

For much of the twentieth century, Roxeth's most prominent — and hated — landmark was the gigantic gas holder, pilloried here in a 1931 cartoon as a memorial to local authority mismanagement. Opened in 1855, the Roxeth Gas Works had originally been a source of both local pride and local employment but it quite literally outgrew its welcome.

Though some attempt was made to camouflage it during the Second World War, the Roxeth gas holder effectively dominated the local skyline from 1931 until its demolition in 1986. It was 240 ft high and 162 ft in diameter, with a capacity of 4 million cubic feet. The large 'NO' on its side apparently informed aircraft that the nearby airport was Northolt not Heathrow.

Rayners Lane, *c.* 1925. As a district, Rayners Lane lacks the history of its neighbour, South Harrow; indeed, at this time it was little more than the charming country lane seen here. Its name is derived from the Rayner family, whose farm was the only building in the lane throughout most of the nineteenth century.

Rayners Farm, Rayners Lane, *c.* 1920. Rayners Farm was acquired for development in 1928 by Metropolitan Railway Country Estates and was soon submerged beneath the houses and shops that typify outer London suburbia. Today, the actual site of the farm house is occupied by nos 404–408 Rayners Lane.

Rayners Lane station, *c*. 1930. With no shelter for its passengers, the first Rayners Lane station, dating from 1906, was known to locals as 'Pneumonia Junction'. In the 1930s bridge-widening work paved the way for the present station which opened in August 1938. The advertisement on the station's roof is for T.F. Nash, the builder responsible for the houses already appearing on the skyline.

Nash Estates Advertisement, Alexandra Avenue, 1934. Probably no one did more to transform Rayners Lane – and, indeed, Kenton and other parts of Harrow – than T.F. Nash, the locally based builder who at his peak employed nearly a thousand workers. In 1934, as part of a major promotion, he erected this triumphal arch at the station end of Alexandra Avenue. (The station can just be seen beneath the arch.)

Odeon Cinema, Rayners Lane, *c*. 1980. Nash also built this cinema at Rayners Lane, currently considered a marvel of thirties architecture and consequently protected from demolition. Although the auditorium itself is no longer used, the front foyers of the building have recently become a 'unique cine-bar experience' under the cinema's original name, The Grosvenor.

Pinner Road, North Harrow. Like Rayners Lane, North Harrow is largely a twentieth-century development which in 1929 acquired a splendid picture palace called the Embassy. In 1963 the cinema was replaced by a supermarket and bowling alley. Hooking Green, the original name for this area, now survives as a cul-de-sac a few minutes walk from this scene.

The first St Peter's Church, West Harrow, *c.* 1912. An early form of prefabrication called *frazzi* was used in the construction in 1907 of the first St Peter's Church designed to serve the fast-growing residential district known as West Harrow. In 1913 this temporary structure was replaced by a larger, more conventional church which in turn became a Christian centre.

Harrow's past and present are most happily linked at Headstone Manor, seen here in about 1925 after centuries as a working farm. The house (centre) was built for the Archbishop of Canterbury in about 1340 and is currently under restoration, while the great barn (left) has been restored appropriately enough for the Harrow Museum and Heritage Centre.